Y0-CZO-987

Getting Started

Getting Started

New Beginnings in the Christian Life

Bill George

All Scripture quotations, unless otherwise indicated, are taken from the Holy Bible: *New International Version* ®. *NIV*®. Copyright © 1973, 1978, 1984 by International Bible Society. Used by permission of Zondervan Publishing House. All rights reserved.

Scripture quotations marked *NKJV* are from the *New King James Version.* Copyright © 1979, 1980, 1982, 1990, 1995, Thomas Nelson, Inc., Publishers.

Scripture quotations marked KJV are from the King James Version of the Bible.

This book is an abridgement of a work published by Pathway Press under the title *What God Expects of Men.* Teachers desiring illustrations to accompany this book may wish to consult the larger book.

Library of Congress Catalog Card Number: 2001117814
ISBN: 0871483750
Copyright © 2001 by Pathway Press
Cleveland, Tennessee 37311
All Rights Reserved
Printed in the United States of America

Dedication

This book is dedicated to my wife

Nelda Davis George

whose delight in life is to help
beginning pastors' wives
achieve success and fulfillment
in their calling.

CONTENTS

INTRODUCTION

"If anyone is in Christ, he is a new creation; the old has gone, the new has come!" exulted Paul in 2 Corinthians 5:17. Anyone who has shared the apostle's discovery of new life knows the joy of new beginnings.

What next? This little book offers practical advice, soundly based on Biblical truth, especially for those who are just getting started in their walk with God or renewing their commitment. It presents in simplicity and order what it means to live a Christian life and how to do it.

As a pastor, missionary and college professor, I have observed numerous new believers successfully put the principles of this book into practice. They will work for you, too.

At the end of each section, I recommend books that go into more detail about the subject. You may wish to purchase some of them for further study. Most are available in local Christian bookstores or may be ordered from Pathway Press, telephone 1-800-553-8506.

I send this book to you with confidence in "him who is able to keep you from falling and to present you before his glorious presence without fault and with great joy" (Jude 24).

—Bill George

CHAPTER 1

WHAT REALLY HAPPENED WHEN I GOT SAVED?

After the first glow of joy and excitement that comes when a new convert realizes he or she is now a child of God, the question arises, "What has happened in my life?"

The purpose of this book is to help you to understand what it means to become a Christian and enable you to better explain to others what happened when Christ came into your heart. People use certain terms to describe their conversion experience and sometimes the terminology is confusing. Some of the key words you will understand better when you have finished this chapter are *redemption, justification, reconciliation and regeneration.*

These words are used to describe the process and results of what we commonly call "getting saved." The Bible advises in 1 Peter 3:15: "Always be prepared to give an answer to everyone who asks you to give the reason for the hope that you have."

Redemption—I'm Redeemed

A hymn we sing uses the expression "I'm redeemed!" A good starting point for understanding what has happened to you is this very word—*redeemed.* It is used commonly in conversations about pawnshops. Suppose a person who owns an expensive watch discovers he needs money. He takes his watch to a pawnshop. The pawnbroker accepts the watch and gives the man a certain amount of money for it. Along with the money, the pawnbroker also gives him a redemption ticket. The customer may return with the ticket, the amount of money he received from the broker for his watch, plus extra money for interest—and buy back his watch. We say he can redeem his watch.

Basically, this is what happens in the life of a person who has become a Christian. Man originally belonged to God. Because God created him and loved him, man was related to God—much as a child is related to his father. Instead of obeying God, however, man chose to turn away from Him and live according to his own desires and wishes. We can think of man as a rebel against God.

Man's choices were bad; they were in conflict with God's will. Man's bad choices, called sin, separate him from God and make him guilty, deserving punishment. Man is unable to pay the price required to make up for his sins. In the opinion of God, only a perfect man could possibly make up for

11

the badness of all men. God, in His love and mercy, provided Someone who could pay the price for man's sin. God gave His only Son, Jesus Christ, who came to earth and lived as a man. Jesus died, even though He was guilty of nothing bad, so that His death could make amends for the sins of every person.

Do you remember how you felt when you grasped the fact that you were a sinner in the eyes of God? How terrible it was to realize that you had no power to do anything to help yourself! You were hopelessly lost! Then it dawned on you that Jesus Christ had paid the price you could not pay! You decided that with His help you would turn away from the sin that separated you from God. When you trusted in Him and what He did on your behalf, then you were saved.

Meaningful words are used in the church to describe what happens. One of these words is *redeemed*, which we have already discussed. When we talk about Christ redeeming us, we mean that He is the One who paid the price for our sin so that we could once again belong to God. This is what Christ said of His own ministry in Mark 10:45: "For even the Son of Man did not come to be served, but to serve, and to give his life as a ransom for many."

Atonement—I'm Right With God

Perhaps you have heard sermons urging the hearers to "get right with God." The Bible uses a beautiful word to express what it means to be right in the eyes of God. It appears often in the Old Testament, but only once in the New Testament (KJV). It is the word *atonement*. Actually it is made up of three smaller words: *at-one-ment.*

God's plan was for humanity to live in harmony with Him and to enjoy fellowship with Him. But God's holy nature cannot tolerate the presence of sin. Sin has come between God and man and has caused separation.

The good news, according to Romans 5:11, is that "we also joy in God through our Lord Jesus Christ, by whom we have now received the atonement" (KJV). When you were saved, you received "at-one-ment." That is to say, you were no longer separated from the presence of God; you were "at one" with Him. Do you remember how you felt when you realized that you were no longer separated from God?

"We . . . joy," the verse says. This means we have reason to be happy. And happiness extends into heaven itself. Luke 15:10 tells us, "There is rejoicing in the presence of the angels of God over one sinner who repents."

12

Peace—I'm at Peace With God

Along with the feelings of joy and happiness comes a deeper emotion which we call peace. *Peace* means "freedom from strife; harmony and concord; an undisturbed state of mind." Paul explains it simply: "We have peace with God through our Lord Jesus Christ" (Romans 5:1).

A vivid word picture of this peace is found in the Bible. In Ephesians 2, Paul discusses the relationship that existed between Jews and non-Jews during the lifetime of Christ. He pointed out that in the Jewish Temple there was a barrier, a wall beyond which Gentiles could not go. They could not enter the inner recesses of the Temple, the area reserved for the Jewish people. Paul thought of this wall as a symbol of the division that exists between men and other men, as well as between men and God. So he said, "For he himself is our peace, who has made the two one and has destroyed the barrier, the dividing wall of hostility" (v. 14). What Christ did when He paid the price for your sin was break down the dividing barrier that existed between you and God.

You have peace when you are saved. There is no fence between you and God!

Justification—The Judge Says, "Not Guilty!"

What has happened to the sins you committed? According to the Bible, the record is clear; you no longer have to answer for those sins.

The word we use to describe this happy state of affairs is *justification.* Paul used this term often. The word comes from the Roman law courts and may be illustrated by a man being brought to court to answer for a crime. Then, for some reason, he does not have to stand trial; he is acquitted. Simply, he is *justified.*

The Word of God says that as a Christian you are justified in the presence of God. Because of what Christ has done, you don't have to go on trial for your sins. Quite literally, *justification* means "just as if I'd never sinned."

Another good way of thinking of justification is to compare it with forgiveness. The two concepts are basically the same. The difference is that *justification* is more of a legal term, whereas *forgiveness* is a more personal concept. For example, you use the legal term *(justification)* when you are thinking of an accused person being acquitted by a judge; you use the more intimate term *(forgiveness)* when you think about pardon being extended by a person who has been offended.

A good discussion of justification in Romans 3:23-26 explains that all men have sinned and come short of what God expects. They need an uprightness they are incapable of producing. But God, through Christ, produces it for them.

Since you have accepted Christ as your Savior, you'll never have to stand before Him when He is judging men to decide if they belong in the kingdom of heaven. In His eyes, you are already declared innocent and set free!

Reconciliation—We're No Longer Enemies

Have you ever started to discuss a mutual friend's divorce action, only to be told, "Oh, haven't you heard the good news? They have reconciled their differences; they're not getting a divorce."

You know what that means. The problem that caused the separation has now been resolved. It has been dealt with and settled and is no longer a factor that will result in divorce.

Reconcile is one of the Bible words that explains what has happened to you. Its other form, *reconciliation*, means "a renewal of friendship." Those who before were enemies and who had differences that hindered their friendship have resolved those problems and are now friends once more. The opposite of *reconcile* is *alienate*. People who cannot, or will not, get along with each other are *alienated*.

Before you were saved, you were alienated from God. Paul describes such people in Ephesians 4:18: "They are darkened in their understanding and separated from the life of God because of the ignorance that is in them due to the hardening of their hearts." He explains reconciliation in Colossians 1:21, 22: "Once you were alienated from God and were enemies in your minds because of your evil behavior. But now he has reconciled you. . . ."

In a nutshell, you are no longer an enemy of God; you are His good friend!

I Can Call Him Father

The clearest picture in the Bible of a sinner who returns to God and is accepted by Him is the story of the prodigal son (Luke 15).

A son asks for his inheritance before his father dies, runs away and wastes all the money. Finally, he returns home broke, hungry and destitute. His father, whom we might have expected to turn him away, welcomes him home and treats him with love, dignity and respect.

This story illustrates God's eagerness to pardon a repentant sinner. It also teaches another equally meaningful lesson: the intimate Father-son relationship that exists between God and His spiritual children.

One of the words the Bible uses to describe this close relationship is *adoption*. Adoption is a word familiar to us today. Prospective parents happily welcome a new child into their home and enter into a parent-child relationship just as if the child had been born to them.

Romans 8:15 explains: "For you did not receive a spirit that makes you a slave again to fear, but you received the Spirit of sonship. And by him we cry , 'Abba, Father.'" *Abba* was an affectionate way of saying "Father" in the language spoken in Palestine in Paul's day. It is similar to the expression "Daddy" we use today.

It means a lot to say you've been adopted into the family of God. When you think about all the implications of being able to call God "Father," you realize just how great it is! Perhaps most amazing of all is that, according to the Bible, when we become His children we also become "heirs of God and co-heirs with Christ" (v. 17).

Regeneration—I've Been Changed

Perhaps the greatest happiness of your Christian experience comes with the knowledge that you've been changed. Think about how the Bible pictures the difference in your old life and your new life.

You are born again. You are born from above. You are a new creation. You have become pure in heart. You are forgiven. You have been made alive. You are a new man. All these expressions signal change.

The change takes place by *regeneration*. It might be helpful to think of regeneration as the divine side of what we call *conversion*, a work of God. We can even say it is a miracle of God. By an act of His favor, He changes the disposition of the soul so that it is renewed in the image of Christ. The sin you once enjoyed now seems awful to you, and you no longer want to engage in it. Sin no longer dominates your life as it once did. Instead, Christ occupies the center of your life.

You have been changed! It wasn't the result of turning over a new leaf; it was the result of turning over a life! It didn't come because of your own wishing and willing; it came because of His great power and His great love. *Regeneration* is just a longer word for what we call the "new birth."

And There's More!

These are just a few of the ways the Bible talks about the wonderful experience that has occurred in your life.

The important truth to grasp is that you are *saved*! *Saved* is the opposite of *lost*; and "lost" described your condition before you were

15

found by Christ. Unhappily, we cannot agree with those people who say that everyone in the world is a child of God and that God is the Father of all. In the sense that He created us, this is true. But the Bible speaks too clearly of the awful consequences of sin and the separation caused by sin, as well as of the redemptive suffering of Christ, for us to treat it lightly or to think of His suffering and death as unnecessary.

You can now sing with all the saints of God the praise hymn that will be sung to Christ in heaven: "With your blood you purchased men for God from every tribe and language and people and nation. You have made them to be a kingdom and priests to serve our God, and they will reign on the earth" (Revelation 5:9, 10).

You can join in the old hymn of the church that says:

Blessed assurance, Jesus is mine!
Oh, what a foretaste of glory divine!
Heir of salvation, purchase of God,
Born of His Spirit, washed in His blood.
This is my story, this is my song,
Praising my Saviour all the day long!
—*Fanny Crosby*

FOR FURTHER STUDY

Little, Paul. *Know What You Believe*. Wheaton, Ill.: Scripture Press Publications, Inc., 1987.

Packer, J.I. *Growing in Christ*. Wheaton, Ill.: Crossway Books, 1994.

Stott, John R.W. *Basic Christianity*. Downers Grove, Ill. InterVarsity Press, 1977.

CHAPTER 2

HE EXPECTS ME TO BE SURE

Suppose someone asked you a few moments after your dramatic saving encounter with Jesus Christ, "Are you saved?" Most likely you would reply, "Oh yes, I'm saved! I feel wonderful!"

That's descriptive, but it's not an adequate answer.

A Christian cannot base the assurance of salvation solely on feelings. New converts sense contentment and joy upon realizing that they have peace with God and the gift of eternal life. But it is equally probable that this newfound happiness will eventually wane and be replaced by depression.

Human emotions are notoriously unreliable and may be compared to a roller coaster—soaring to the heights of elation, then plummeting to the depths of despair. Doctors say that certain mood changes can result from improper diet. The lack of certain food elements in the body may cause temporary feelings of depression. How foolish, then, to let emotions control your sense of spiritual well-being.

If you can't trust your feelings, how can you be sure that you are saved? Many Christians say that they have been strengthened at this point by a consideration of the Book of 1 John.

John explained to first-century Christians and to us why he wrote the epistle: "I write these things to you who believe in the name of the Son of God so that you may know that you have eternal life" (5:13). As one of the 12 disciples of Jesus, he stressed the idea that Christians can know certain spiritual truths without doubt. The word *know* (or a form of the word) appears more than 30 times in the brief Book of 1 John. The Holy Spirit can also speak to you and help you to find assurance of your salvation through the words He inspired 20 centuries ago.

Believing His Word

God has revealed certain basic truths in His Word. You would do well to commit these basic scriptures to memory.

Christ received you. "All that the Father gives me will come to me, and whoever comes to me I will never drive away" (John 6:37).

Christ holds you always and won't turn loose. "I give them eternal life, and they shall never perish; no one can snatch them out of my hand" (John 10:28).

17

Christ will never abandon you. "God has said, 'Never will I leave you; never will I forsake you.' So we say with confidence, 'The Lord is my helper; I will not be afraid. What can man do to me?'" (Hebrews 13:5, 6).

Christ forgives you when you sin and He cleanses you. "If we confess our sins, he is faithful and just and will forgive us our sins and purify us from all unrighteousness" (1 John 1:9).

Christ provides a way out of temptation. "No temptation has seized you except what is common to man. And God is faithful; he will not let you be tempted beyond what you can bear. But when you are tempted, he will also provide a way out so that you can stand up under it" (1 Corinthians 10:13).

All these Scripture verses are facts. If a time comes when you don't "feel" saved, you may even begin to doubt whether you really exercised faith. When these experiences occur, recall these verses and tell God, the devil, and everybody else that this is God's Word and you are going to stand on it!

Keeping His Commandments

Basing your experience on the facts of God's Word is the surest way to know you are saved. But it is not the only way. John says, "We know that we have come to know him if we obey his commands" (1 John 2:3).

Jesus placed great importance on His followers' obeying His commandments. On the night before He was crucified, He told His disciples that He was not going to refer to them as servants anymore, but as friends. Then He added, "You are my friends if you do what I command" (John 15:14).

This business of obeying Christ makes sense. He has come to the earth to set up His kingdom. Anytime people live together, there is a need for rules and standards to govern conduct. If we lived in a world where everyone obeyed God's will, it would be an ideal world—no crime, poverty, war or any of the factors that mar human relationships. Only when we get to heaven will we live in that kind of world. In the meantime, the Lord wants us to be a model of the kind of citizens who will inhabit His kingdom.

When you are born again, your new nature wants to live His kind of life. There is something within you that urges you to make the right choices. It checks you when you make a wrong choice. John puts it this way: "We know

18

that we have come to know him if we obey his commands" (1 John 2:3).

When you have the spirit of Christ in your life, you don't want to do wrong constantly. Instead, you are driven to repentant prayer when you realize that you have displeased your Lord. This desire to keep His commands is one of the ways you know you are saved.

Loving the Brethren

John mentions another proof of our salvation in 1 John 3:17-20: "If anyone has material possessions and sees his brother in need but has no pity on him, how can the love of God be in him? Dear children, let us not love with words or tongue but with actions and in truth. This then is how we know that we belong to the truth, and how we set our hearts at rest in his presence whenever our hearts condemn us."

This kind of love is characterized by a willingness to "lay down our lives" and sacrifice personal good for the benefit of another. This is an altogether rare and unnatural quality in today's what's-in-it-for-me kind of world.

Jesus told His friends that when they obeyed His commands and went out of their way to minister to others, it was as though they had done it personally to Him (see Matthew 25:40).

Receiving the Spirit

One of the more satisfying assurances of your salvation is the fact that the Holy Spirit lives in you. In 1 John 4:13, John puts it this way: "We know that we live in him and he in us, because he has given us of his Spirit."

The Bible teaches that salvation is a work of the Spirit: He performs the new birth; He testifies of Christ in your life. The Christians in the New Testament set a pattern in their experience, however, which lets us know that a constant fullness may be added to the indwelling of the Spirit. After He has done His work of redemption, the Holy Spirit will come to the believer in an empowering baptism to equip him for service. If you are a Christian, if you are obeying your Lord, and if you fervently desire His presence in your life, you may receive this baptism of power.

The fact of His arrival and His ministry in your life will be a constant reminder that, indeed, you are a child of God.

19

FOR FURTHER STUDY

Marshall, I. Howard. *Pocket Guide to Christian Beliefs.* Downers Grove, Ill.: InterVarsity Press, 1991.

Rhea, Homer. *A New Creation.* Cleveland, TN: Pathway Press, 1996.

CHAPTER 3

HE EXPECTS ME TO CONFRONT TEMPTATION SUCCESSFULLY

After you were saved, if you thought, "Thank God! Now that I've given my heart to the Lord, I am through with sin," you were wrong. As a matter of fact, it is likely that you now notice temptations to sin even more than before you were converted.

Everyone is tempted to sin. Simon Peter, who was one of the original Twelve and later a leader in the church, wrote to his fellow believers: "Dear friends, do not be surprised at the painful trial you are suffering, as though something strange were happening to you" (1 Peter 4:12). He was saying to them—and to you: temptation is inevitable.

Satan's business is to tempt God's people. He began his work in the Garden of Eden by deceiving Eve, and he has been successfully tempting people ever since.

The first step you should take in dealing with temptation, then, is to acknowledge that it is going to come. As surely as day follows night, temptation will follow your encounter with God. It was true in the experience of Jesus himself. One of the most powerful spiritual occurrences of His life was His baptism, when the Spirit descended in the form of a dove and the Father spoke aloud to His Son. But what happened immediately afterward? The Bible says, "Then Jesus was led by the Spirit into the desert to be tempted by the devil" (Matthew 4:1).

What Temptation Is

Let's be sure at the outset that we are talking about the same thing when we use the word *temptation*.

Temptation is an incitement of natural desires to go beyond the bounds God has set. Almost always, temptation has to do with normal, God-given desires and inclinations that are not sinful when gratified as God intended.

When you indulge yourself, strive to obtain things and do things outside of God's desire for you, then it is sin. It is the mission of Satan, the tempter, to incite you to give in to wrong desires or gratify natural desires in wrong ways.

Help! I'm Being Tempted!

To overcome temptation successfully, you must resist it. In James 4:7, God gives assurance: "Resist the devil, and he will flee from you." The Bible pictures the devil as a roaring lion, prowling around and looking for someone to devour (1 Peter 5:8); but in the same passage believers are told to resist him (v. 9). Would God tell you to do something that is impossible to do?

The Bible also teaches: "No temptation has seized you except what is common to man. And God is faithful; he will not let you be tempted beyond what you can bear. But when you are tempted, he will also provide a way out so that you can stand up under it" (1 Corinthians 10:13).

Admit that if you really want to sin, you are going do it. It's only when you want to live a holy life that you will resist temptation. Your identification with Christ, then, lies at the heart of victory over sin. If He lives in you, you will not want to do anything contrary to His will. If you find yourself doubting, slipping, unsure, leaning toward un-Christlike desires, turn to Him for strength and guidance.

At times you may be uncertain about whether a course of action is sinful or not. God's Word doesn't give lists of what is sin and what is not, although it does make clear certain sinful practices. It also spells out principles that you can apply. Ask yourself certain questions when you are confronted with temptation:

- Will this action bring glory to God?
- If Jesus were in my place, would He do it?
- Can I ask God to bless me in doing it?
- Will this action hurt or offend anyone?
- Would I want to be found doing this when Christ returns?

The answers that the Holy Spirit brings to your mind will help you to decide the right course of action.

Getting Ready to Face the Devil

If temptation is a sure thing in the life of a Christian, how can you prepare yourself for the battle? Again, the Bible gives instructions and examples for guidance.

Your primary weapon against the devil is the strength and power of the Word of God.

"How can a young man keep his way pure?" asks the psalmist; and he immediately answers: "By living according to your [God's] word" (Psalm 119:9). Then, in verse 11 he adds, "I have hidden your word in my heart that I might not sin against you." Someone once wrote in the front of his Bible, "Sin will keep you from this Book, but this Book will keep you from sin."

Consider this revealing information about Jesus: "For we do not have a high priest who is unable to sympathize with our weaknesses, but we have one who has been tempted in every way, just as we are—yet was without sin" (Hebrews 4:15). The pattern Jesus set in winning over temptation in the wilderness—quoting the Bible to get rid of the tempter—was the method He used when He was tempted "in every way, just as we are." It is wise to stay out of places where you might reasonably expect to confront temptation, but if you find yourself confronted by it, you can wield the sword of the Spirit, which is the Word of God, just as Jesus did, and win the victory over the devil.

The Spirit's Role

You may find it somewhat confusing to read that temptation is a work of the devil and then encounter statements that God, or the Spirit of God, has something to do with it. How can we reconcile this apparent contradiction?

It is certain that all experiences and circumstances in the life of a Christian are under the control of the Father. The apostle Paul told about a trying circumstance in his life (see 2 Corinthians 12) he referred to as a "thorn in the flesh" and a "messenger of Satan." He ascribed his temptation to the devil. Yet, he recognized that God had the power to take away the thorn. While we understand that no prompting to sin comes from God, we also recognize that God sometimes permits such trials in order to accomplish His own purposes.

God sends us trials to make us better; the Enemy sends us temptations to destroy us. James gives us this example:

> Consider it pure joy, my brothers, whenever you face trials of many kinds, because you know that the testing of your faith develops perseverance. Perseverance must finish its work so that you may be mature and complete,

23

not lacking anything. . . . Blessed is the man who perseveres under trial, because when he has stood the test, he will receive the crown of life that God has promised to those who love him (1:2-4, 12).

God may permit the devil to tempt you, but rest assured that He will never allow you to be tempted beyond your capacity to endure and overcome. Using the Word of God as a spiritual weapon, you can defeat the devil.

And If I Fail . . . ?

What happens if, despite all your efforts to resist, you fall into sin? Run quickly back to Jesus! The powerful message of 1 John 1:9 is, "If we confess our sins, he is faithful and just and will forgive us our sins, and purify us from all unrighteousness." First John 2:1, 2 explains that God doesn't want us to sin; but if we do, we have an Advocate, Christ Jesus, who will plead our case in God's presence.

FOR FURTHER STUDY

Anderson, Neil. *The Bondage Breaker.* Eugene, Ore.: Harvest House
Publishers, 1992.

CHAPTER 4

HE EXPECTS ME TO KNOW HIS WORD

A father bought his 4-year-old son a Christmas present. He chose a little pedal car which came unassembled with all the parts packed in a box. On Christmas Eve, after the boy was asleep, the father began to put the car together. Much to his dismay, he discovered the manufacturer had packed the wrong instructions with the car. The company, which produced other wheeled items, had mistakenly included directions for assembling a baby carriage instead of the pedal car. What should have taken only 30 minutes developed into a four-hour project, because he had to work without directions.

The Bible is God's instruction book. In it you will find directions for living a Christian life.

How Should I Think of the Bible?

Looking at it objectively, the Bible is a collection of 66 books and letters, written by about 40 authors over a span of perhaps 16 centuries. It contains poetry, history, biography, sermons and predictions of future events.

But the Bible is more. It is the Word of God. Man is able to understand many things by science and reason, but the best way he can learn things about God is for God to reveal them to him. The Bible contains God's revelation of Himself.

The Bible, then, is a very special book. No other book has the weight of authority the Bible has. It is divinely inspired; that is, the human authors who penned the words of the Bible were guided by God as they wrote. The message of the Book is a message from God. Peter put it this way: "For prophecy never had its origin in the will of man, but men spoke from God as they were carried along by the Holy Spirit" (2 Peter 1:21). Paul wrote: "All Scripture is God-breathed and is useful for teaching, rebuking, correcting and training in righteousness, so that the man of God may be thoroughly equipped for every good work" (2 Timothy 3:16).

The majesty of the Bible, its great length, and the awe that it inspires have caused some new Christians to fear to open it for study. Your reaction should be just the opposite! God has revealed truths about Himself, about man, about sin, about creation and about many other subjects. He revealed these truths precisely because He wants us to learn them.

Incidentally, it will be helpful if you realize that the Bible can be read in a relatively short time. While a serious course of Bible study will take longer, it has been proven that the average reader can read from Genesis to Revelation in about 80 hours.

It Looks So Complex!

The person who opens the Scriptures for the first time is confronted with an index page that lists columns of strange-sounding names. Divided into two sections, the first and longer column is called the Old Testament, and the shorter column is called the New Testament. *Testament* means "covenant"—or, as we would say today, "agreement." The Old Testament is the account of people who lived under an old type of agreement with God, and the New Testament reveals God's new agreement with mankind through Jesus Christ.

The names of the 66 books seem somewhat strange because they come from forms of languages that no longer exist. The Old Testament was written mostly in Hebrew with a few passages in Aramaic. The New Testament writers used Greek. (Modern Hebrew and Greek languages are different from the forms used in the Bible.)

Open your Bible to the index page and let us look at the list of books.

Old Testament

The first five—Genesis, Exodus, Leviticus, Numbers and Deuteronomy—are called the Books of the Law. They are called this because a large part of their content is the law of God as given to Moses—including, for example, the Ten Commandments. These books begin with the story of Creation and continue until the death of Moses. Fascinating stories are told about such persons as Adam, Noah, Abraham, Isaac, Jacob, Joseph and Moses.

The next 12 books (Joshua through Esther) are traditionally referred to as the Historical Books, called this because they record the history of the Jewish people.

Job, Psalms, Proverbs, Ecclesiastes and the Song of Solomon are categorized as the Poetic Books or Wisdom Literature.

The remaining 17 books in the Old Testament, the Prophetic Books, record the sermons and messages of prophets. The first five are referred to as the Major Prophets, and the other 12 are called the Minor Prophets. This does not reflect on the importance of their work, but only the relative length of their writings.

New Testament

The New Testament contains four Gospels, one history book, 21 letters and one prophecy book.

The Gospels—Matthew, Mark, Luke and John—relate facts about the life and teachings of Christ. Acts is a history book that catalogs some of the story of the church from about A.D. 30 to A.D. 60. Of the 21 Epistles ("letters"), at least 13 (perhaps 14) were written by the apostle Paul. Seven (or eight) were composed by other church leaders. These letters were originally written to churches and individuals to give them guidance, instruction and encouragement. The last book, Revelation, is dedicated principally to predictions of events to take place in the future.

How Can I Study?

The following ideas are important if you wish to gain the greatest benefit from reading the Bible:

1. *Read the Bible daily.* Just as your body needs regular meals in order to stay strong, you also need the Word of God to remain spiritually healthy.

2. *Pray before you read.* Ask the Holy Spirit to open your mind and to help you to understand what God wants to say to you.

3. *Read in a pattern.* That is, don't just let the Book fall open and begin reading. Select a book of the Bible and read it through on successive days.

4. *Start with easier parts of the Bible first.* Many readers find that Mark or John is a good place to begin. The Psalms are also helpful and easy to read.

5. *Use a good version.* There are dozens of versions of the Bible. Some are translations, and some are paraphrases. A translation is produced directly from Hebrew and Greek manuscripts and attempts to convey exactly what the text says. A paraphrase, on the other hand, attempts to say basically the same thing, but in language arranged for ease of understanding. The most widely accepted version of the Bible is the King James Version, translated in 1611. Readers discover that the meanings of some words have changed and that the style of this version is not exactly the way we talk today. For beauty and majesty of language, however, the King James Version is unsurpassed and is a trustworthy, reliable translation. A good recent translation is the *New International Version*, which is used in this

book. Other good ones are the *New King James Version* and the *New Living Translation.* Some versions have been translated by people who do not believe the Bible to be inspired; therefore, changes have sometimes been made that alter the meaning. Ask someone who is familiar with the versions before you purchase one.

6. *Look for a personal message in your reading.* That is, ask yourself, "What does God want to say to me in this passage?"

7. *Keep a notebook.* When you discover a truth that is meaningful for you, write it down.

8. *Read with a plan.* With the help of a mature friend, decide on a course of study that will take you through the whole Bible, book by book.

FOR FURTHER STUDY

Arthur, Kay. *How to Study Your Bible.* Eugene, Ore.: Harvest House Publishers, 1994.

Mears, Henrietta C. *What the Bible Is All About.* Glendale, Calif.: Regal Books, 1987.

CHAPTER 5

HE EXPECTS ME TO COMMUNICATE WITH HIM

It is amazing that the Creator of the universe has issued a standing invitation to every believer to come into His presence at will, but this is exactly the case. The inspired writer of Hebrews says, "Let us then approach the throne of grace with confidence, so that we may receive mercy and find grace to help us in our time of need" (4:16). The means by which you communicate with God is prayer.

The key scripture for this chapter is Matthew 16:9-13. Take the time to read it before going farther. The Bible outlines the conditions under which God hears and answers prayer. It also records examples of the results of prayer.

Benefits of Prayer

Prayer ensures certain benefits to the child of God.

Prayer delivers from trouble. "'Because he loves me,' says the Lord, 'I will rescue him; I will protect him, for he acknowledges my name. He will call upon me, and I will answer him; I will be with him in trouble, I will deliver him and honor him'" (Psalm 91:14, 15).

Prayer delivers from temptation. "Watch and pray so that you will not fall into temptation. The spirit is willing, but the body is weak" (Matthew 26:41).

Prayer brings joy to the believer. "Ask and you will receive, and your joy will be complete" (John 16:24).

Prayer supplies needs. "The poor and needy search for water, but there is none; their tongues are parched with thirst. But I the Lord will answer them; I, the God of Israel, will not forsake them" (Isaiah 41:17).

Prayer provides communion with God. "I love those who love me, and those who seek me find me" (Proverbs 8:17).

Conditions of Successful Prayer

The Bible makes it clear that certain conditions must prevail if you are to expect positive responses to your prayers.

Faith. Jesus told His disciples, "Whatever you ask for in prayer, believe that you have received it, and it will be yours" (Mark 11:24). The opposite of faith is unbelief, and unbelief has often hindered the work of Christ.

Matthew explains, "And he [Jesus] did not do many miracles there because of their lack of faith" (13:58). Your attitude must be one of trust in God's power and in His willingness to answer your prayers.

Obedience. We read these assuring words: "Dear friends, if our hearts do not condemn us, we have confidence before God and receive from him anything we ask, because we obey his commands and do what pleases him" (1 John 3:21, 22). An attitude of unwillingness to obey God's commands results in God's disapproval. An Old Testament example is found in 1 Samuel 15. Take a moment and read it. Saul was rejected as king over God's people because he refused to obey God.

Righteousness. Psalm 66:18, 19 puts it rather bluntly: "If I had cherished sin in my heart, the Lord would not have listened; but God has surely listened and heard my voice in prayer." A New Testament example is equally plain: "The prayer of a righteous man is powerful and effective" (James 5:16). A man who has not rejected a sinning lifestyle cannot expect to remain in communion with a holy God.

Wholeheartedness. The testimony of Scripture is this: "You will seek me and find me when you seek me with all your heart" (Jeremiah 29:13). On the other hand, a stern warning goes out to those who treat lightly the things of God and who choose not to fear the Lord. About these, God says, "They will call to me but I will not answer; they will look for me but will not find me" (Proverbs 1:28).

Spiritual praying. There is abundant Biblical evidence that God is not impressed with long, carefully worded, elaborate, repetitious prayers (see Matthew 6:7; 23:14, KJV). What touches the heart of God is an earnest, intense cry from the heart of His child. At times you might not understand the exact way you ought to pray. The words you need won't come. At such times, the Holy Spirit will pray through you and for you.

This passage explains this ministry of the Spirit: "The Spirit helps us in our weakness. We do not know what we ought to pray for, but the Spirit himself intercedes for . . . the saints in accordance with God's will" (Romans 8:26, 27).

Even though you don't know the direction your prayer ought to go, the indwelling Spirit of God does know, and He prays for you. In your times of prayer, yield to Him and allow Him to perform His prayer ministry through you.

A Model Prayer

Jesus' disciples were concerned about prayer. They observed their Lord's habit of spending time alone with God, and one day they petitioned Him, "Lord, teach us to pray" (Luke 11:1). His answer to their request was to give them a model prayer. We often refer to it as the Lord's Prayer. Let's look at the elements of this prayer that was first given to teach believers how to pray. Perhaps you can gain insights that will help your own developing prayer life. (You can read the prayer in Matthew 6:9-13 and Luke 11:2-4.)

"Our Father in heaven." The prayer begins with a recognition of the fact that a Father-child relationship exists between God and His people. Believers can now enter into the presence of God as a child enters the presence of his earthly father.

"Hallowed be your name." One of the aims of true prayer is worship and adoration. When you pray, you should spend time at the beginning of your prayer giving glory and honor to the Father.

"Your kingdom come." Christ came to set up a Kingdom, and He has begun it by changing the lives of people so that they can be fit citizens of that Kingdom. In this part of the prayer, request that Jesus' kingdom will come soon. Always pray in the spirit of John, recorded in the closing verses of the Book of Revelation, "Even so, come, Lord Jesus" (22:20, KJV).

"Your will be done on earth as it is in heaven." This aspect of the prayer is a request for God to have His way in the affairs of this world.

"Give us today our daily bread." When you pray, you are acknowledging your dependence on a higher power. This part of the model prayer lets us know that we can depend on our Father for spiritual blessings and material provision.

"Forgive us our debts." Just as bread is the basic physical necessity, so forgiveness is the basic spiritual necessity. We should always enter into God's presence conscious of how we fall short of the holiness of God. We should always approach Him with the plea on our lips that He will forgive those shortcomings.

"Lead us not into temptation, but deliver us from the evil one." God has the power of protecting us from the evil of this world. Jesus teaches us to depend on the Father for deliverance from the traps and temptations of Satan.

The King James Version includes a beautiful ascription of praise to close the prayer: "For thine is the kingdom, and the power, and the glory, for ever. Amen" (Matthew 6:13).

31

FOR FURTHER STUDY

Arthur, Kay. *Lord, Teach Me to Pray in 28 Days*. Eugene, Ore.: Harvest House Publishers, 1995.

Blackaby, Henry. *Experiencing God*. Nashville, Tenn.: Broadman/ Holman, 1994.

Bounds, E.M. *Power Through Prayer.* Grand Rapids: Baker Books, 1992.

Triplett, Bennie S. *Praying Effectively.* Cleveland, Tenn.: Pathway Press, 1990.

CHAPTER 6

HE EXPECTS ME TO BE FILLED WITH THE SPIRIT

Salvation is the greatest spiritual experience anyone can have. Once you are saved, however, it is the will of God for you to be baptized with the Holy Spirit. Learning what the Bible says about the Holy Spirit will lead you into new depths in your experience with God.

Every saved person is *indwelt* by the Holy Spirit, but the Bible also teaches that it is possible to be *filled* with the Spirit. This filling is an experience separate and apart from conversion.

What the Bible Teaches

The disciples were saved, but they were baptized in the Spirit seven weeks after Jesus returned to heaven. A large number of people in Samaria were converted under the ministry of Philip. Later, when Peter and John visited them, they received the Holy Spirit. Paul had a marvelous conversion encounter on the road to Damascus; three days later he was filled with the Spirit. Many years elapsed between the conversion of some former disciples of John and the time they received the Spirit, but it happened. These examples from Acts 2, 8, 9 and 19 set the Biblical pattern: First, you are saved; subsequently (it may be in moments, days, or years) you receive the infilling of the Spirit.

The Spirit's Ministry

Why is the baptism in the Holy Spirit provided for believers? The Scriptures teach us about certain ministries He fulfills in our lives.

1. *The Spirit empowers for service.* "But you will receive power when the Holy Spirit comes on you; and you will be my witnesses in Jerusalem, and in all Judea and Samaria, and to the ends of the earth" (Acts 1:8).

2. *The Spirit guides and directs.* On various occasions, according to the Bible, the Holy Spirit gave directions to the church and to individual Christians. Here is one example:

"Paul and his companions traveled throughout the region of Phrygia and Galatia, having been kept by the Holy Spirit from preaching the word in the province of Asia" (Acts 16:6).

This is in fulfillment of Christ's words in John 16:13: "But when he, the Spirit of truth, comes, he will guide you into all truth. He will not speak on his own; he will speak only what he hears, and he will tell you what is yet to come."

3. *The Spirit teaches.* Jesus shares another promise relating to this aspect of the work of the Spirit: "But the Counselor, the Holy Spirit, whom the Father will send in my name, will teach you all things and will remind you of everything I have said to you" (John 14:26). This means that our spiritual eyes are opened so we can see divine truths. With this reliable Teacher filling our being, we can grasp with greater clarity the significance of what the Bible says.

4. *The Spirit prays.* At times we don't understand how we ought to pray. At such times, the Spirit within literally prays for us:

"In the same way, the Spirit helps us in our weakness. We do not know what we ought to pray for, but the Spirit himself intercedes for us with groans that words cannot express. And he who searches our hearts knows the mind of the Spirit, because the Spirit intercedes for the saints in accordance with God's will" (Romans 8:26, 27).

5. *The Spirit gives gifts.* To ensure the success and effectiveness of the church, God has promised to give special capabilities to its members. These capabilities are of divine origin, and the Bible calls them spiritual gifts. There are a number of these gifts. Part of the ministry of the Spirit is to distribute these gifts among the members of the church (see 1 Corinthians 12).

6. *The Spirit helps.* The Holy Spirit is called *Helper (NKJV), Counselor (NIV),* and *Comforter* and *Advocate* (KJV). These words are translated from the Greek word *paraclete.* No one word is capable of conveying the exact meaning of paraclete. It literally means "one who comes alongside to help." The Holy Spirit comes to help, whatever the nature of the help we need. He comes alongside to help us in ways we recognize and in ways we may never know.

How to Receive

How do believers receive this Baptism?

1. *He fills clean lives.* The primary requirement for receiving the baptism of the Holy Spirit is that your life be changed by the new birth and cleansed by the sanctifying power of Christ. In all the cases in the New Testament, the individuals who were baptized in the Spirit first responded to the gospel with saving faith; only then did they receive the Spirit.

2. *He fills those who desire Him.* The Holy Spirit does not come uninvited or unwanted. While it is the Father's great desire to equip all His

children and to dwell in their lives through His Spirit, He waits until His presence is sought; He never intrudes.

Jesus taught His followers: "If you then, though you are evil, know how to give good gifts to your children, how much more will your Father in heaven give the Holy Spirit to those who ask him!" (Luke 11:13).

3. *He fills obedient Christians.* In defending his preaching of the gospel before a Jewish court, Simon Peter—who was Spirit-filled on the Day of Pentecost—injected a little-noticed statement: "We are witnesses of these things, and so is the Holy Spirit, whom God has given to those who obey him" (Acts 5:32). Obedience, said Peter, is one of the characteristics of the person who desires to receive the Spirit. Obeying Christ, in simplest terms, means doing what He said.

4. *He fills those who have faith.* "He redeemed us in order that . . . by faith we might receive the promise of the Spirit" (Galatians 3:14). Some people try to "earn" the Spirit by good works, by spiritual exercises, by making bargains with God. All He asks, however, is that you meet the conditions of a sanctified life, be hungry for His presence, and be obedient to His will. Then, when you accept His Spirit just as you accepted salvation— by faith—He will fill you.

The Evidence

This was a normative New Testament experience. In every case where a person or group received the baptism of the Spirit, the Bible either clearly says or strongly implies that the evidence of the infilling was speaking in tongues. Thousands of individuals in today's Christian community who have experienced the same witness testify to its truth.

FOR FURTHER STUDY

Black, Daniel. *A Layman's Guide to the Holy Spirit.* Cleveland, Tenn.: Pathway Press, 1988.

Horton, Stanley. *What the Bible Says About the Holy Spirit.* Springfield, Mo.: Gospel Publishing House, 1995.

Hughes, Ray H. *Who Is the Holy Ghost?* Cleveland, Tenn.: Pathway Press, 1992.

Lowery, T.L. *The Baptism of the Holy Ghost.* Washington, D.C.: Lowery Ministries International, n.d.

CHAPTER 7

HE EXPECTS ME TO KNOW AND DO HIS WILL

God has made arrangements for you to know and do His will. Certain signs will let you know what He wants you to do in your Christian life and service.

Dozens of Biblical examples may be found of individuals whose lives were chosen by God to accomplish a meaningful purpose. Abraham was set apart to be the father of the Hebrew nation. Joseph told his brothers who had sold him into slavery: "You meant it for evil, but God meant it for good" (see Genesis 50:20). Moses was raised up to deliver the Israelites from Egyptian slavery. Samuel was called to keep the knowledge of God alive in his day. As you read the Bible, you will be able to recognize many other examples of people who were chosen to perform certain tasks.

These are examples of specific guidance, but in the lives of many individuals, the will of God may not be spelled out in detail. God seems to give His children a great deal of latitude in determining the exact shape of His will for them. The important condition is that we are always in His moral will— obeying His commandments and not contradicting anything He has told us.

When we speak of doing the will of God, we generally refer to the life purpose of an individual. We may also be talking about a calling to special, full-time service. One of the first questions to ask yourself is, "Does God want me to dedicate my life to full-time service?" Several signals will help you find the answer to this question.

First, if the Lord means for you to give your life to a ministry such as preaching or missions, He will call you to this ministry. The call comes to different people in different, but distinct, ways. A few report dramatic emotional encounters where they see visions or hear voices, but this is rare. Usually the call is perceived as an inner impression. You begin to feel a strong desire to fulfill a certain ministry—perhaps preaching. You pray about it and ask God to make it clear, and still the feeling persists. Over a period of weeks and months, it does not wane; it intensifies. You feel you must preach or die!

This internal witness is generally a strong indication of God's will. Occasionally, however, it is merely a reflection of genuine admiration the believer may have for those who occupy these ministries. There will be other indications as well.

How does the church think of you? In the New Testament, the church was sometimes the agency used by the Holy Spirit to choose ministers. Acts 13:1-3 gives an account of individuals identified for special Christian service by means of the church. It is generally true that if you sense an inner witness that God wishes you to serve Him in Christian vocation, your brothers and sisters in the church will confirm the calling. If they voice strong doubts or counsel you to proceed slowly, it is a good idea to consider their advice.

God's enablements may be thought of as a third sign of your calling. If God wants you to fulfill a certain ministry, He will equip you to perform it. If He wants you to become a missionary, for example, it is likely He will give you the ability to study and to learn a foreign language. He will equip you with special gifts or capabilities you will need to fulfill the ministry. God will also begin to open doors through which you may enter as you actually begin your ministry.

These three indications, then, will help you know if the Lord wishes you to serve Him full-time: (1) You will sense an undeniable urge, or calling, within your heart; (2) the church will more than likely confirm the calling; and (3) you will recognize certain divine helps as you prepare to fulfill your ministry.

God's Will for All

Only a relatively small percentage of Christians receive a calling to vocational service. The majority discover that God wishes them to serve Him in what we normally call "secular" work. This may mean that you will work as a factory employee, a nurse, a teacher, a mechanic, a waitress—or in any one of thousands of other jobs. What God expects of us all, however, is faithfulness to Him in whatever we do. He wants us to be closely related to Him so that we may be led by Him.

Jesus told a crowd of listeners, "Not everyone who says to me, 'Lord, Lord,' will enter the kingdom of heaven, but only he who does the will of my Father who is in heaven" (Matthew 7:21). A short time later He said, "For whoever does the will of my Father in heaven is my brother and sister and mother" (12:50). It is not just words that are effective in establishing a relationship with Him; rather, what interests Him most is the direction our life takes.

In the Garden of Eden, Adam, faced with a choice, took a selfish course, saying in effect, "I will do what I want." But Jesus, faced with a choice in the Garden of Gethsemane, said, "Not what I will, but what you [God] will"

(Mark 14:35). Jesus gave us His personal example to teach us perfect submission to the Father's will.

Steps to Follow

The first step in discovering God's will is a surrendered life. Psalm 40:8 voices the sentiments of a consecrated man: "I desire to do your will, O my God; your law is within my heart." One follows the other: A man can desire God's will only when his heart is right with God.

Perhaps the best-known call for a surrendered life in Scripture is Romans 12:1: "Therefore, I urge you, brothers, in view of God's mercy, to offer your bodies as living sacrifices, holy and pleasing to God—this is your spiritual act of worship." The result of offering yourself is explained in verse 2: "Then you will be able to test and approve what God's will is—his good, pleasing and perfect will."

The second step is prayer. Scripture records instances of people praying and seeking divine direction. Psalm 143:10 is such a petition: "Teach me to do your will, for you are my God."

The third step is obedience. While God's complete plan for your whole life will not be unfolded all at once, it is certain that He will reveal some aspects of His will as you study the Bible and pray. For instance, there are clear indications of God's will in the following instructions:

"It is God's will that you should be sanctified: that you should avoid sexual immorality; that each of you should learn to control his own body in a way that is holy and honorable" (1 Thessalonians 4:3).

"Be joyful always; pray continually; give thanks in all circumstances, for this is God's will for you in Christ Jesus" (1 Thessalonians 5:16-18).

And There Are Rewards

We must not suppose that this matter of knowing and doing God's will is the beginning of a road of suffering and affliction; quiet the opposite is the case. It is true that at times the will of God may entail difficulties. The will of God for His Son led Him to a cross. For Paul it included shipwreck. But there are awesome rewards when you discover God's will and do it.

First, you establish a unique, intimate personal relationship with Jesus Christ. He told the people of His day, "My . . . brothers and those who hear God's word and put it into practice" (Luke 8:21).

Second, you place yourself in a position where you can learn more about God. You will gain spiritual discernment. Jesus said, "If anyone chooses to do God's will, he will find out whether my teaching comes from God or whether I speak on my own" (John 7:17).

Finally, fulfilling the will of God in your life guarantees a right standing before God throughout eternity. Scripture lets us know: "The world and its desires pass away, but the man who does the will of God lives forever" (1 John 2:17).

To know and to do God's will is worth the necessary investment of time, energy, prayer and consecration.

CHAPTER 8

HE EXPECTS ME TO WITNESS

Each believer has the privilege and responsibility to cooperate with the Lord in spreading the good news of the gospel throughout the earth. When we come to the end of life, our greatest legacy will be those who live eternally because we shared our faith with them.

To the men whom He had called and who had committed themselves to Him, Jesus gave final instructions just before He returned to the Father. He told them: "Go and make disciples of all nations, baptizing them in the name of the Father and of the Son and of the Holy Spirit, and teaching them to obey everything I have commanded you. And surely I am with you always, to the very end of the age" (Matthew 28:19, 20).

He added pointedly, "But you will receive power when the Holy Spirit comes on you; and you will be my witnesses" (Acts 1:8).

Some people might read these verses and suppose that only the 12 disciples were to be involved in representing Christ to the world. But this ministry calls for the participation of all Christians. One of the plainest statements of this truth is 2 Corinthians 5:17-20:

> Therefore, if anyone is in Christ, he is a new creation; the old has gone, the new has come! All this is from God, who reconciled us to himself through Christ and gave us the ministry of reconciliation: that God was reconciling the world to himself in Christ, not counting men's sins against them. And he has committed to us the message of reconciliation. We are therefore Christ's ambassadors, as though God were making his appeal through us. We implore you on Christ's behalf: Be reconciled to God.

This passage uses the word *ambassador*, which we still use in government language today. An ambassador is one empowered and commissioned to represent his head of government in a foreign land. We are here on earth representing our divine head, Jesus Christ, who resides in heaven. These verses make clear, too, the nature of our work as ambassadors. We are to be engaged in the work of reconciliation, which means we bring men into a right relationship with God, from whom they are separated by sin.

Once you became a Christian and committed yourself to obey and serve the Lord, you became His witness.

How Can I Witness?

You may be like many other Christians who want to be witnesses but are not sure how to go about it. Paul Little, in his book *How to Give Away Your Faith*, shares some helpful suggestions. These are based on an encounter that Jesus had with a woman of Samaria, as told in John 4.

1. *Get to know people.* Jesus approached a public well at about the same time as did a woman from the community. He didn't avoid meeting her; as a matter of fact, He initiated a conversation.

We, too, need to make it our business to get to know unsaved people. If we don't make contacts among non-Christians, we will not make converts. Look for ways to establish friendships. While it is admirable to live a life separated from sin, it is wrong to separate yourself completely from nonbelievers.

2. *Talk about things that interest the other person.* In His interview with the Samaritan woman, Christ began their conversation by talking about water, because she had come to get water from the well. We need to look for something that interests the other person so we can talk on common ground.

3. *Try to stimulate interest.* One of the best textbooks on witnessing is James Kennedy's *Evangelism Explosion.* It contains a simple outline of the gospel, which the witnessing encounter should ultimately include. Kennedy suggests the use of two questions. The first one asks, "Have you come to the place in your spiritual life where you know that if you were to die tonight, you would go to heaven?" A second question follows: "If you stood in the presence of God and He asked you, 'Why should I permit you to enter heaven?' what would you answer?" The two queries penetrate to the heart of the issue of salvation and how a person is saved.

Another method suggests the use of several leading questions about family, occupation and religion, which stimulate interest in spiritual things and lead up to the gospel presentation.

4. *Don't rush a decision.* Sometimes, in our eagerness to get our unsaved acquaintances to make a spiritual decision, we ride roughshod over their feelings, even to the point of making ourselves unwelcome in the future.

Remember that conversion is not a human work; it is a spiritual matter. The Holy Spirit is the One who ultimately convicts a sinner of sin and convinces him to turn to Christ. We need to discover the fine balance between presenting the gospel, with its demands and urgency, and harshly pressing acceptance.

5. *Be positive.* A common error in witnessing is to come down hard on the vices and bad habits of the person to whom you are testifying. We know that God condemns immorality and unclean living; consequently, there is a tendency to crusade for reform. But remember that the call of Christ is not to quit smoking and drinking—His call is "Come to the Cross." The sanctified life follows conversion; it doesn't precede it.

Good advice, then, is not to condemn and blame, but rather to present a message of hope. The old proverb, "You catch more flies with honey than with vinegar" can be applied directly to your witnessing attitude.

6. *Don't debate.* The Samaritan woman began to feel uncomfortable in the presence of Christ, so she endeavored to change the subject to something controversial—a religious question. Jesus deftly answered the question and came right back to the heart of her problem.

People invariably bring up foolish questions, such as, "Where did Cain get his wife?" Or they attempt to spotlight doctrinal differences among denominations in order to change the subject. This is usually because they feel uncomfortable about their own personal spiritual condition. A good rule is try not to get sidetracked.

7. *Press for an answer.* This is the other side of number 4. While it is true that you should not try to force a person against his will, neither should you leave a neutral impression. The claims of Christ deserve and require an answer. Impress upon the person that he cannot remain forever in the valley of decision as far as Christ is concerned; in his mind and will, he must decide one way or another.

Be careful to grasp the significance of the distinction between pressing for an answer and forcing a decision. Don't rush the question, but underline the fact that one cannot be neutral about the most important questions of eternity.

God Gets People Ready

Before Paul ever spoke the first word of faith-sharing in the city of Corinth, God assured him, "I have many people in this city" (Acts 18:10). The assurance God was giving His servant was that He was going before the apostle and getting people ready to receive and respond to the message he would bring. God works on the other person's heart to receive the message even before He works on you to share it.

Witnessing Expects Results

When the Lord left instructions for us to go and witness, it was with the expectation of results.

"You did not choose me, but I chose you and appointed you to go and bear fruit—fruit that will last" (John 15:16). Shortly afterward He prayed that the Father would be with all His followers: "My prayer is not for them alone. I pray also for those who will believe in me through their message" (17:20). Jesus believed that when His followers witnessed, they would gain converts.

Closely akin to the matter of witnessing is the subject of workers for the spiritual harvest. To help us understand the nature of our task, Jesus compared the unsaved people of the world to a great field of grain ready to be reaped. He counseled, "The harvest is plentiful but the workers are few. Ask the Lord of the harvest, therefore, to send out workers into his harvest field" (Matthew 9:37, 38). Part of your efforts to win people, then, will go beyond your direct personal testimony and will involve praying to the Father to send still more workers who will also try to win people.

We must witness and pray for more witnesses. Jesus has no other plan.

FOR FURTHER STUDY

Adist, Christopher. *Personal Disciple Making*. Laguna Hills, Calif.: Here's Life Publishers,

Kennedy, D. James. *Evangelism Explosion*. Wheaton, Ill.: Tyndale House Publishers, 1983.

Little, Paul E. *How to Give Away Your Faith*. Downers Grove, Ill.: InterVarsity Press, 1988.

Strobel, Lee. *Inside the Mind of Unchurched Harry and Mary*. Grand Rapids: Zondervan, 1993.

Sustar, T. David. *Transforming Faith*. Cleveland, Tenn.: Pathway Press, 1992.

CHAPTER 9

HE EXPECTS ME TO EXERCISE STEWARDSHIP

A part of God's original plan for man was for him to manage what God entrusted to him. In Creation, God placed man in the midst of all He made and told him to rule over it. Indeed, man was to rule over everything but himself (Genesis 1—3).

Stewardship, according to Scripture, entails a great deal more than just the management of money—although that is probably the most readily observable aspect of stewardship. The apostle Peter captured the broader meaning of stewardship when he wrote: "Each one should use whatever gift he has received to serve others, faithfully administering God's grace in its various forms" (1 Peter 4:10). Paul was also talking about more than money when he observed: "Now it is required that those who have been given a trust must prove faithful" (1 Corinthians 4:2).

From earliest times, money management has figured into the relationship man has enjoyed with God. Long before Moses gave the people the Law he received from God, some men had begun the practice of dedicating a tenth of their income in worship. Abraham began the tithe (*tithe* literally means "the tenth part"). Jacob confirmed the practice, and the Law established it. "The tithe . . . is the Lord's" (Leviticus 27:30, KJV). Giving up material possessions seems always to have been a mark of reverence and devotion to God.

The Bible Gives Direction

Throughout the Old Testament, men continued to bring the tithe to God, both before the giving of the Mosaic Law and afterward. The closing page of the Old Testament contains a succinct, easily understood order and promise from God to His people: "'Bring the whole tithe into the storehouse, that there may be food in my house. Test me in this,' says the Lord Almighty, 'and see if I will not throw open the floodgates of heaven and pour out so much blessing that you will not have room enough for it'" (Malachi 3:10).

The practice of tithing continued in the time of Christ and was sanctioned by Him. He openly objected to some religious traditions of the Pharisees; but when He mentioned their custom of exercising great care that their tithe not be neglected, He said, "You are right . . . you should have done this; but you should not have neglected weightier matters like justice, mercy, and faithfulness" (Matthew 23:23, paraphrased).

Systematic, regular, percentage-related giving was taught by Paul to the members of churches he established. He urged each Christian to set aside a sum of money on the first day of each week according to his income (1 Corinthians 16:2).

Guidelines for Giving

By reading the New Testament teachings of Jesus about material possessions, we can learn what our attitude and manner of giving should be.

While ministering on earth, Jesus was interested in how people gave to God. In Mark 12:41 we read: "Jesus sat down opposite the place where the offerings were put and watched the crowd putting their money into the temple treasury." He demonstrated genuine interest in the relative amounts people gave. This Biblical passage is the one where Jesus commended a widow who gave a tiny offering, because it constituted all she had.

Two truths stand out in this account:

1. Jesus takes note of what you give.

2. The measure of an offering is not how much you give, but rather how much you have left after you have given. Jesus pointed out, "They all gave out of their wealth; but she, out of her poverty, put in everything—all she had to live on" (v. 44).

The Lord is also concerned about the heart attitude with which you give. In our day, as in His, some people give just to receive a pat on the back. He talked about seeing men announce their offerings and gifts to the needy with trumpet blasts! They do it, He explained, "to be honored by men. . . . But when you give to the needy, do not let your left hand know what your right hand is doing, so that your giving may be in secret" (Matthew 6:2, 3). He concluded by promising that "your Father, who sees what is done in secret, will reward you [openly]" (v. 4).

The matter of rewards for giving is also prominent in the Bible. Paul counseled Christians: "Remember this: Whoever sows sparingly will also reap sparingly, and whoever sows generously will also reap generously" (2 Corinthians 9:6). Jesus himself emphasized this same point when He urged liberal giving in Luke 6:38: "Give, and it will be given to you. A good measure, pressed down, shaken together and running over, will be poured into your lap. For with the measure you use, it will be measured to you."

Giving is also noted by the Father. When Cornelius received an angelic visitor who told him to send for Simon Peter, the angel informed him, "Your prayers and gifts to the poor have come up as a memorial offering before God" (Acts 10:4). He and his whole household were subsequently saved and filled with the Spirit as a result of his faithfulness and obedience to God.

Why Is Giving So Important?

The Bible dedicates a great deal of space to stewardship. Why? Probably because the management of possessions may be one of the best public testimonies of what really is inside the heart.

A number of parables and true stories teach us negative aspects of the money questions. Jesus taught a lesson about the rich fool—called this because he gave a great deal of attention to money and possessions and completely ignored the spiritual side of his life (see Luke 12:13-21). Acts 5 recounts the death of Ananias and Sapphira, a couple in the Jerusalem church who lied to the leaders of the congregation about a money matter. In 1 Timothy 6:10 is a stern warning about attaching undue affection to worldly possessions: "For the love of money is a root of all kinds of evil. Some people, eager for money, have wandered from the faith and pierced themselves with many griefs." Dozens of exhortations in the New Testament concern the proper attitude toward the proper management of money.

One of the best-known of the Lord's parables concerns the Good Samaritan. He is so named because he invested his time and money in a poor, hurt traveler who desperately needed assistance (Luke 10:25-37).

The parables of the hidden treasure and the pearl of great price (Matthew 13:44-46) teach us about proper values. The parable of the 10 talents (Matthew 25:14-30) teaches accountability. The story of the unjust steward (Luke 16:1-10) teaches trustworthiness. The list could continue. Jesus taught that you can recognize a tree by the fruit it bears. In the same way, you announce to the world—and to God—a great deal about yourself by the way you exercise stewardship.

FOR FURTHER STUDY

Burkett, Larry. *How to Manage Your Money.* Chicago: Moody Press, 1993.
Ronsvale, Sylvia. *Behind Stained Glass Windows.* Grand Rapids: Baker Books, 1996.
Taylor, Al. *Proving God.* Cleveland, Tenn.: Pathway Press, 1991.

CHAPTER 10

HE EXPECTS ME TO BE PART OF HIS CHURCH

The word *church* appears in the New Testament more than 100 times. Its origin is a Greek word *(ekklesia)* that can be literally translated "called-out ones." It refers to a group of people assembled for a particular purpose.

This is the designation chosen by Jesus himself for His people. In Matthew 16:18, He announced: "I will build my church, and the gates of Hades [hell] will not overcome [prove stronger than] it."

Theologians have written long, involved definitions of what the church is, but the following statement sums up the most important aspects: *The church is a group of redeemed people banded together for worship, study, fellowship, care and evangelism.*

The church has a special relationship with the Father. It is called God's building, His household, His temple, His people and His city. It has special relationship with the Son, because it is called His bride, His body, His branches and His flock. He called it "my church." The church also has a special relationship with the Holy Spirit because He constitutes the church, He empowers it and He guides its leaders and members.

What Is the Church For?

The church exists to perform Christ's work in the world. The Scriptures teach a number of different functions of the church, but most of them fit in one of the following five categories.

1. *Worship.* God desires His people to worship Him. One of the most beautiful scenes of heaven, depicted in the Book of Revelation, shows a worshiping multitude in the presence of God. They sing, "You are worthy, our Lord and God, to receive glory and honor and power" (4:11).

The church brings God's people together for corporate worship, when brothers and sisters join their voices in prayer and song to God.

2. *Evangelism.* The church is the center of soulwinning activity. The Book of Acts serves as a brief history of the first 30 years of the church. The picture that emerges can serve as a pattern for our day—a church that was unashamedly evangelistic in outreach.

A typical church in New Testament times encouraged its members to reach out into nearby communities and preach, win converts and plant churches. The new church would repeat the pattern, reaching local people and pushing out to a new community, constantly growing.

God's plan for His church today is the same.

3. *Education.* In an earlier lesson we learned that the Lord left His church definite instructions, which we call the Great Commission, found in Matthew 28:18-20. Pulling the command verbs out of verses 19 and 20, we come up with the words "Go . . . make disciples . . . baptizing . . . teaching." In Greek, all these verbs are in participle form, except the one that says "make disciples." Therefore, the verbs can literally read, "Going, baptizing, teaching—make disciples." "Make disciples" is the heart of the marching orders.

A disciple is one who follows another in order to learn from him. Christ's followers were called disciples. He still calls us to come to Him in order to learn. "Take my yoke upon you and learn from me," He invites in Matthew 11:29.

The church functions to help its members learn spiritual truths. Through its agencies, such as Sunday school and midweek Bible training, the church guides us through organized programs of study that encompass all of the Bible and cover all areas of Christian living.

4. *Caring.* The New Testament knows nothing of "Lone Ranger" Christianity. Believers manifest care for their brothers and sisters, as well as for those who are outside the family of faith. Caring marks Christians as models of Christ's love.

5. *Fellowship.* There is strength in unity. A poetic passage in the Old Testament expresses it this way: "Two are better than one, because they have a good return for their work: If one falls down, his friend can help him up. But pity the man who falls and has no one to help him up! . . . Though one may be overpowered, two can defend themselves. A cord of three strands is not quickly broken" (Ecclesiastes 4:9-12).

The New Testament church is characterized by unity and fellowship: "They devoted themselves to the apostles' teaching and to the fellowship, to the breaking of bread and to prayer. . . . Every day they continued to meet together in the temple courts. They broke bread in their homes and ate together with glad and sincere hearts, praising God and enjoying the favor of all the people" (Acts 2:42, 46, 47). This kind of quality time spent together with the people of God is a foretaste of the unity that heaven promises.

These five aspects of the church's activity—worship, evangelism, education, caring and fellowship—encompass the purposes of the church.

The Church and Its Government

The church is made up of local congregations who, together, form a worldwide fellowship. In the Church of God, the officers include pastors and overseers who coordinate the work of the church on district, state or regional and international levels.

The doctrines and teachings of the church are expressed in the Declaration of Faith and in a list of teachings and practices taken from the Bible. When believers become members of the church, they hear these statements read and promise to live by them.

The church celebrates three ordinances taught by Scripture: water baptism, the Lord's Supper and footwashing.

God's View of the Church

God expressed a high opinion of His church, inspiring Peter to write: "You are a chosen people, a royal priesthood, a holy nation, a people belonging to God, that you may declare the praises of him who called you out of darkness into his wonderful light. Once you were not a people, but now you are the people of God" (1 Peter 2:9, 10).

God sees the church as a victorious union. Some men and women throughout history have been quick to discount the church. They have predicted its decease and demise. But it still lives. It is alive and well. Born in a blaze of Pentecostal fire, it survives intact and powerful today—20 centuries later. However, the church is always just one generation from extinction. Consequently, we must carefully study what the Bible says about the church, then prayerfully and sincerely commit ourselves to upholding its purposes and doctrines.

When Jesus comes back, He is coming for His church.

FOR FURTHER STUDY

Chapman, Mike. *Church Membership*. Cleveland, Tenn.: Pathway Press, 1994.

Colkmire, Lance. *Welcome to the Family*. Cleveland, Tenn.: Pathway Press, 1994.

George, Bill. *Added to the Church*. Cleveland, Tenn.: Pathway Press, 1987.

CHAPTER 11

HE EXPECTS ME TO USE MY SPIRITUAL GIFTS

Every Christian has been endowed by his Lord with certain abilities that enable him to serve God and mankind better. We call these endowments "spiritual gifts." They are "spiritual" because they are of divine origin and "gifts" because they are freely bestowed.

Like most Christians, you may ponder at times the great task confronting the church and wonder how we, as weak human beings, can possibly hope to accomplish the work we have been given. The answer is found in recognizing that the same Lord who charges the church to win and teach the world also equips its members to perform the mission. This equipment comes in the form of spiritual gifts.

What Are Spiritual Gifts?

A Scriptural study of gifts reveals that God has indeed made provision for each believer to utilize special abilities that enable him to fulfill his call to service in the Kingdom. The word ability indicates capacity to do effective work. It suggests the idea that Christians, by reason of their gifts, are qualified and strengthened to satisfy the responsibilities God has given them.

Who Has Spiritual Gifts?

The New Testament teaches that every one of us has received a gift or gifts. The following Scripture passages support this claim:

"But to each one of us grace has been given as Christ apportioned it. This is why it says: 'When he ascended on high, he led captives in his train and gave gifts to men'" (Ephesians 4:7, 8).

"Now to each one the manifestation of the Spirit is given for the common good. . . . All these are the work of one and the same Spirit, and he gives them to each one, just as he determines" (1 Corinthians 12:7, 11).

These and other verses make it clear that the gifts are not reserved for favored people with above-average natural abilities—they are for all.

How Many Gifts Are There?

Many good books about spiritual gifts have been written by Christian authors. An interesting phenomenon is that these books suggest a wide variety in the number of gifts the Bible indicates are available. Some suggest that certain gifts ceased a few decades after Christ first gave them (an idea unsupported by the Bible). Some count nine gifts; others count 18, 19, 27 or 30. There are repetitions in the lists given in the New Testament. Although gifts are mentioned in various passages, there are five principal lists.

- Romans 12:6-8
- 1 Corinthians 12:6-10
- 1 Corinthians 12:28
- Ephesians 4:11
- 1 Peter 4:11

These lists contain duplications and perhaps overlap. They do not include other gifts mentioned in other settings or demonstrated by other examples—such as the gift of celibacy, missionary and hospitality, to name a few. Some Christians believe the Scriptural designations are general and there may be room for other specific gifts besides those named. However, they suggest that any God-given endowment that equips a person for service and edifies the body of Christ might be considered a spiritual gift.

Is there a distinction between spiritual gifts and natural talents? An essential difference seems to be that anyone—Christian or not—may possess talents. Talents, generally, are apparent in the unconverted as well as the converted, and they are not necessarily used for spiritual edification. For example, some outstanding college professors who can captivate their audiences as they teach are men and women far from God. Their ability is a talent for teaching.

On the other hand, a spiritual gift seems to date from conversion. It is given for spiritual service and is exercised to serve and edify others.

How Can I Discover My Gift?

You can do several things to find out what spiritual gift or gifts God has given you. You can also learn how to use your gift to benefit the kingdom of God and bring glory to the Giver.

1. *Pray.* "Do not be anxious about anything, but in everything, by prayer and petition, with thanksgiving, present your requests to God" (Philippians 4:6). This counsel from Paul tells us that we are not to worry about discovering our spiritual gifts; rather, we are to ask God to show us. "We have not, because we ask not" is as true today as when James wrote it 2,000 years ago (see James 4:2, KJV).

2. *Study the possibilities.* Read the passages in the Bible concerning

spiritual gifts, considering the various gifts along with your own personality, desires and feelings. Realize that two or more gifts frequently seem to be combined in the lives of individuals. For example, a man may have the gift of teaching and, at the same time, also have the gift of encouragement. (Barnabas seems to be an example of this gift combination.)

3. *Act on faith.* Once you have made the question of your gift a matter of prayer, act on the impressions you receive. If God has equipped you to serve Him, He will not wish to keep it a secret from you! This then is a suggestion: If you believe you may have the gift of teaching, try teaching. (Understand, however, that not all gifts are subject to this kind of experimentation.)

4. *Obey the Spirit.* The Holy Spirit distributes the various gifts according to the grace of God. In explaining how the members of the church work together to accomplish the desired purpose, the Bible compares the church to a human body, each part serving its particular function. In 1 Corinthians 12:18, Paul makes it clear that "God has arranged the parts in the body, every one of them, just as he wanted them to be."

If God, by His Spirit, has dispensed gifts throughout the church, He will allow His Spirit to lead each one to the proper exercise of His gift.

FOR FURTHER STUDY

Chapman, Mike. *Developing Your Spiritual Gifts.* Cleveland, Tenn.: Church of God Lay Ministries, 1993.

Sustar, T. David. *A Layman's Guide to the Fruit of the Spirit.* Cleveland, Tenn.: Pathway Press, 1990.

Wagner, C. Peter. *Your Spiritual Gifts Can Help Your Church Grow.* Glendale, Calif.: Regal Books, 1994

CHAPTER 12

HE EXPECTS ME TO EXPECT HIM

You, as a Christian, are heir to what the Bible calls "the blessed hope." This "hope" refers to the doctrine of the second coming of Christ.

The return of Christ signals the consummation of history as we know it. It will be the reality for which Christians have long waited, prayed and hoped. This hope is one of the strongest incentives to live a holy life and seek to perform God's will.

What We Already Have

God has made rich provisions for His people. Someone has counted more than 30,000 promises in the Bible. When we add up the statements of blessing we have been assured of, it is almost unbelievable. Despite the fact that we are subject to difficulties, temptations, accidents and sickness, the advantages of being a Christian—even if measured only in terms of this life—easily outweigh whatever disadvantages someone may claim.

- We have peace with God.
- We have the satisfaction of knowing that our sin has been covered and our guilt taken away.
- We have the assurance of forgiveness.
- We have received the Holy Spirit.
- We can live in harmony with others.
- Our needs are being supplied.
- We can boldly approach the Father to request healing when sickness comes.
- We know that we will be given divine direction.

Promise mounts upon promise to prove to the world that we are, of all people, most blessed. It is no wonder that words like *joy, peace, love* and *happiness* are frequently heard in the vocabulary of the Christian.

But this is not all. Paul stated: "If only for this life we have hope in Christ, we are to be pitied more than all men" (1 Corinthians 15:19). Thank God, there is more. Everything in Scripture points to it and everything within us cries out for it. *God is not finished with us in this life.* The ultimate revelation of God to His people will be when Jesus comes back to earth.

He Promised He Would Come

Jesus frequently told His disciples He would come again. In one of His last discussions with them, He told them He was going away to the Father's house to prepare a place for them. "And if I go and prepare a place for you, I will come back and take you to be with me that you also may be where I am," He promised (John 14:3).

Someone has counted more than 300 references to the Second Coming in the pages of the New Testament. These teachings fall most often from the lips of Jesus himself, but it is a doctrine common to all the writers. Paul frequently mentioned and explored the theme. It was prominent in the sermons preached by the apostles, including Peter. According to Acts 1:11, angels renewed the promise Jesus had already made to the disciples. Jude predicted it. John anticipated it.

He Tells Why He Will Come

In the last chapter of the Bible, where the promise to return is repeated three times, Jesus indicates part of the purpose for His coming back: "Behold, I am coming soon! My reward is with me, and I will give to everyone according to what he has done. I am the Alpha and the Omega, the First and the Last, the Beginning and the End" (Revelation 22:12, 13). In these verses are definitive reasons why He will return. At the heart of the matter is the fact that He will reward His people.

If your experience has been typical, you have encountered people who doubt the gospel. There are some who believe the content of the Bible has been fabricated by men. To the multitudes who openly believe this—and to many others who live as if they believe it—Jesus' coming will be the final proof of the truth of God's revelation. When Jesus says that He is the Alpha and Omega, He literally means that in Him dwells the completeness of God's making Himself known. (Alpha and omega are the first and last letters of the Greek alphabet; they are like A and Z in the English language.) According to John 1:1-3, Jesus was in the beginning, and all things were made by him; He will also be at the ending when all things will be climaxed by Him.

His coming will show the world the Bible is true, good ultimately overcomes evil and there is moral order in the universe God created.

He Tells How He Will Come

Beginning readers of the Bible are sometimes puzzled by two seemingly contradictory statements that predict the coming of Christ. First Thessalonians 5:2 says He will come as a thief in the night, while Matthew 24:27 indicates that His coming will be like lightning that flashes across the sky. How can you reconcile these two opposite statements?

Other Biblical passages shed light on the matter. The message of 1 Thessalonians 4:13-18 is one of the best explanations of Christ's coming as a thief in the night:

> Brothers, we do not want you to be ignorant about those who fall asleep, or to grieve like the rest of men, who have no hope. We believe that Jesus died and rose again and so we believe that God will bring with Jesus those who have fallen asleep in him. According to the Lord's own word, we tell you that we who are still alive, who are left till the coming of the Lord, will certainly not precede those who have fallen asleep. For the Lord himself will come down from heaven, with a loud command, with the voice of the archangel and with the trumpet call of God, and the dead in Christ will rise first. After that, we who are still alive and are left will be caught up together with them in the clouds to meet the Lord in the air. And so we will be with the Lord forever. Therefore encourage each other with these words.

His coming will be like the coming of a thief only in that it will be totally unexpected and will occur suddenly. It will take the world by surprise. The event described here is sometimes called the Rapture, a word that captures the idea expressed by the phrase "caught up" in verse 17. Christ will appear in the air and will draw to Himself all Christians who have ever lived or who are now alive.

The "caught up" Christian will meet the Lord and return to heaven with Him. After a period of celebration and peace in His presence, Christ will return, this time all the way to the earth. With an army at His side, He will defeat—for time and eternity—the Evil One. This activity of His coming is like the lightning, for all the world will see it.

What Happens Then?

We have never seen the world as God made it and as He intended it to be. Our world is under a curse of sin that settled over it when man rebelled against God's lordship. This curse has affected all of nature.

Christ's second coming initiates a new world order. We can look beyond His coming to the final triumph it makes possible. Peace, that has for centuries eluded the desires and efforts of good men, is achieved. A blessed world ministers to its inhabitants. The gates of the city of God are opened, giving access to the Tree of Life.

The closing pages of the Bible paint a beautiful picture. We will hunger or thirst no more. There will be no tears. His servants shall see His face.

Peter realized the tremendous spiritual value that the knowledge of the Second Coming would give to each Christian: "Since everything will be destroyed in this way, what kind of people ought you to be? You ought to live holy and godly lives as you look forward to the day of God and speed its coming" (2 Peter 3:11, 12).

FOR FURTHER STUDY

Britt, George. *When Dust Shall Sing.* Cleveland, Tenn.: Pathway Press, 1985.

Buxton, Clyne W. *End Times.* Cleveland, Tenn.: Pathway Press, 1993.